CINCINNATI
BENGALS

KENNY ABDO

Fly!
An Imprint of Abdo Zoom
abdobooks.com

abdobooks.com

Published by Abdo Zoom, a division of ABDO, P.O. Box 398166, Minneapolis,
Minnesota 55439. Copyright © 2022 by Abdo Consulting Group, Inc. International
copyrights reserved in all countries. No part of this book may be reproduced in any
form without written permission from the publisher. Fly!™ is a trademark and logo
of Abdo Zoom.

Printed in the United States of America, North Mankato, Minnesota.
052021
092021

Photo Credits: Alamy, AP Images, iStock, Shutterstock PREMIER
Production Contributors: Kenny Abdo, Jennie Forsberg, Grace Hansen
Design Contributors: Candice Keimig, Neil Klinepier

Library of Congress Control Number: 2020919485

Publisher's Cataloging-in-Publication Data

Names: Abdo, Kenny, author.
Title: Cincinnati Bengals / by Kenny Abdo
Description: Minneapolis, Minnesota : Abdo Zoom, 2022 | Series: NFL teams |
      Includes online resources and index.
Identifiers: ISBN 9781098224578 (lib. bdg.) | ISBN 9781098225513 (ebook) |
      ISBN 9781098225988 (Read-to-Me ebook)
Subjects: LCSH: Cincinnati Bengals (Football team)--Juvenile literature. | National
      Football League--Juvenile literature. | Football teams--Juvenile literature. |
      American football--Juvenile literature. | Professional sports--Juvenile literature.
Classification: DDC 796.33264--dc23

TABLE OF CONTENTS

CINCINNATI BENGALS

The Cincinnati Bengals have torn up football fields for years to make it to many NFL **championships**.

Their signature chant "Who Dey?" and mascot not only unite Bengal fans, but the city as a whole.

KICK OFF

The Bengals were founded by Paul
Brown in 1967. The team began play
in the American Football League
(AFL) in 1968.

Brown named Cincinnati's team the Bengals in 1968. This was the name of an AFL team that played in the city from 1937 to 1942.

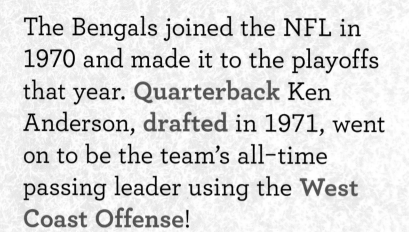

The Bengals joined the NFL in 1970 and made it to the playoffs that year. **Quarterback** Ken Anderson, **drafted** in 1971, went on to be the team's all-time passing leader using the **West Coast Offense**!

TEAM
RECAPS

The Bengals made it to **Super Bowl** XVI and XXIII! Unfortunately, they lost both games to the San Francisco 49ers.

The Bengals had few victories from 1991 to 2004. However, in 2005, the Bengals finally had their first winning season in 15 years. They also won the **division** title.

Quarterback Andy Dalton and wide receiver A.J. Green joined the team during the 2011 season. They were considered to be one of the greatest passing duos in the game.

Despite their success, the Bengals lost the Wild Card Playoffs to the Texans, 31-10.

For the 2019 season, the Bengals hired Zac Taylor as head coach. Sadly, they were still the first team to be cut from playoff competition in week 11, ending with a 2-14 season.

For the 2020 season, the team managed to grab the #1 overall 2020 **draft** pick Joe Burrow as **QB**. Unfortunately, his **rookie** season ended midway with an injury. The Bengals ended the season with a miserable 4-11-1 record.

HALL OF FAME

Ken Riley played with the Bengals for 15 seasons. He caught 65 **interceptions** throughout his career, a Bengals team record. Riley played in 207 games, another team record.

During the 2011 season, **rookie** Andy Dalton passed for more than 3,000 yards. He is one of five rookie QBs to do that. Dalton is the only **quarterback** on the Bengals to catch a touchdown.

A.J. Green joined the Bengals during the 2011 season. He is the only Bengal to play at the Pro Bowl in each of his first five seasons. Between 2011 and 2013, Green caught more than 260 passes. That was more than any other player in NFL history at the time.

GLOSSARY

championship – a game held to find a first-place winner.

division – a group of teams who compete against each other for a championship.

draft – a process in sports to assign athletes to a certain team.

interception – when a player catches a pass that was meant for the other team's player.

quarterback (QB) – the player on the offensive team that directs teammates in their play.

rookie – a first-year player in a professional sport.

Super Bowl – the NFL championship game, played once a year.

West Coast Offense – offense that is based on passing, instead of running.

ONLINE RESOURCES

Booklinks
NONFICTION NETWORK
FREE! ONLINE NONFICTION RESOURCES

To learn more about the
Cincinnati Bengals, please
visit abdobooklinks.com
or scan this QR code.
These links are routinely
monitored and updated to
provide the most current
information available.

INDEX